CARIBBEAN SECURITY THREATS

A threat assessment for islands of the Caribbean

Orlando "Andy" Wilson

Orlando "Andy" Wilson

"If something can corrupt you, you're corrupted already"

BOB MARLEY

CONTENTS

This book was written while I was in Saint Lucia in June 2019 running a protective surveillance and hostile environment awareness course with RPS Group OECS Inc. and the Institute of Security and Public Safety of Saint Lucia.

THE CARIBBEAN

Most people's view of the Caribbean and its more than 7,000 individual islands is that of a tropical paradise: blue seas, white sand beaches, and palm trees. To some extent this is accurate, but what most tourists and visitors either don't see or are prevented from seeing is the real situation.

The Caribbean has always been and continues to be a haven for smugglers and pirates. Historically the islands have traded amongst themselves and what is classed as drug trafficking routes today are nothing more than the old trade routes. The contraband used to be rum and tobacco; nowadays it has been replaced by drugs, firearms and dirty money.

In many ways the methods used by the traffickers today are pretty much the same as they were in the 1700s, what has changed is the designs of the boats they use and the inclusion of light aircraft. The multitude of islands in the Caribbean have the same porous borders they had 300 years ago.

What has changed greatly, even in the past few decades is the economy within the Caribbean. It is now largely based on tourism, which is not a stable industry, instead of agriculture. The tourism within the Caribbean can be negatively affected by various factors from many different angles: natural disasters, hurricanes, high-crime, terrorism, increases in aviation fuel prices or difficulties in the home economies of the tourists themselves.

In addition to tourism, many of the islands have ventured into the offshore financial sector which in some locations is booming. The US and some European countries are critical of the offshore banking and financial service sectors in the Caribbean due to their excessive secrecy and lack of transparency which raise money laundering concerns. But what is the alternative for these countries since their traditional industries, like agriculture, have disappeared?

Also, what a lot of tourists and visitors don't see from their all-inclusive resorts and luxury villas is the high rate of unemployment and poverty that plague many of the islands. Such matters could be a major destabilizing factor in the future.

In this short book, we aim to educate readers by highlighting some of the issues within the Caribbean as well as offer suggestions on how to ensure stability in a potentially unstable region.

Orlando "Andy" Wilson

REGIONAL THREATS

Human Trafficking

Typically, when human trafficking is discussed, most of the focus is the wellbeing of the supposed victims. The very real threat of terrorists or organized criminals mixing in with those being trafficked is ignored. The Islands within the Caribbean are vulnerable to all types of trafficking due to their penetrable borders and lack of maritime security infrastructure. The general understanding of human trafficking within Latin America and the Caribbean is that those being trafficked have the goal of reaching the United States. However, many are seeking to establish themselves in the Caribbean.

Human Trafficking is a gateway crime. Initially, those being trafficked will have to pay for their passage to their country of choice. For example, the current rates for Haitians wanting to be trafficked to say Dominica is $5000.00 USD. In addition to their human cargos, many of the boats are also carrying drugs and firearms.

The economic impact of human trafficking also needs to be taken into consideration. In many areas throughout the Caribbean there are communities of immigrants who have entered illegally, have established themselves, took jobs from the locals and send most of their earnings back to their home countries rather than reinvesting in the local economy. This, in turn, has a negative effect on the overall economy of the host country.

On many Islands throughout the Caribbean, it is possible for illegal immigrants and those with money to buy the documents required to obtain residency and work permits in the countries of their choice. In one location we will not name in order to protect our source's security, passports are issued to illegal immigrants, for a fee from their embassy, and they are then directed to corrupt local immigration officials who will stamp their new passports with the required visas etc. From an international security perspective, this means criminals can assume new identities, access passports, and travel documents. Immigration officials and those that can influence the immigration processes are prime targets for criminals and organized crime groups to try to corrupt.

Many of those being trafficked are far from being the innocent victims they like to portray to law enforcement and the media when they are caught. Throughout the Caribbean women from the Dominican Republic are renowned for setting up prostitution rings. The Venezuelan gangs that are spreading out over the region are bringing with them drugs, kidnapping, and violence.

As I said earlier, human trafficking is a gateway crime that brings with it criminals who seek to establish themselves and exploit the communities they embed themselves in.

Narco-Trafficking

According to the United Nations, illegal drug trafficking within the Caribbean is an industry worth $3.3 billion U.S. dollars annually. Cocaine from South America flows into the Caribbean from Venezuela and Guyana via sea and air to be sold in the Islands or transported to the US and Europe. Marijuana grown within the Caribbean is traded internally amongst the Islands and also to drug traffickers from Venezuela etc. in exchange for cocaine, firearms, and ammunition.

Illegal drugs are easily transported around the Caribbean on a multitude of maritime vessels ranging from fishing boats, oil tankers and freighters to luxury yachts that roam between the Islands. The issues for Customs Services and Coast Guards are to try to identify suspicious vessels and then conduct thorough searches with limited resources and time. Illegal drug shipments into Europe, the U.S. and Africa are also facilitated via commercial maritime vessels and private yachts.

In addition to concealing illegal drugs on maritime vessels and amongst their cargo the drug gangs also use human "mules" that swallow capsules of drugs. The creativity of the drug gangs has led them to the commercialization of the guts of the Corvina fish. The digestive system of that fish is extremely resistant, and the criminals use their guts to make little capsules to carry cocaine thru a "mule".

In the past "Mules" swallowed capsules made of latex. When they would have a meal, the latex materials would react with the gastric juices which resulted in the latex capsules exploding, and the "mules" dying of poisoning. This represented a high financial loss to the gangs. The solution to the problem was "The Buche" or guts of the Corvina, which are resistant to gastric juices, flexible and prevent the drugs being contaminated.

A kilo of these guts is very expensive within Venezuela. There have been multiple gunfights and killings between rival gangs in an effort to gain control of the commercialization of Corvina guts as it is a very profitable business.

At a more sophisticated level, it is common for drug deliveries to be airdropped into the sea to be retrieved by fishing boats or divers. The light aircraft from Venezuela drop the drugs at pre-arranged GPS coordinates to be picked up by waiting fishing boats or the drugs are weighted down and retrieved later by divers. The drugs are then transported ashore hidden in or under the fishing or dive boats to be sold locally or to continue being trafficked to their final destination.

Arms Trafficking

In the Northern Caribbean, the supplies of illegal firearms and ammunition predominantly flow south out of the United States on commercial and private maritime vessels, whereas in the Southern Caribbean illegal arms are flowing north from Venezuela.

As with the illegal drug trafficking trade, firearms and ammunition are easily transported around the Caribbean Islands via a multitude of maritime vessels. Illegal firearms and ammunition are often concealed within commercial goods ranging from bags of rice to motor vehicles. The vast amounts of merchandise being shipped into the Caribbean from the United States alone means local Customs Services cannot search the majority of the cargo being imported to their countries.

In addition to the commercially bought small arms (pistols/rifles) coming out of the United States, the threat from military grade medium weapons (light anti-armor weapons, etc.) coming out of such places as Venezuela is very real.

With strict firearms laws within the Caribbean, the demand for illegal firearms and ammunition by criminals is high. Those seeking to legally own firearms for sporting and self-defense purposes usually face lengthy in-depth vetting procedures.

Terrorism

At this point acts of terrorism are extremely rare within the Caribbean but there is a high potential for future incidents. It's common knowledge that citizens from Trinidad and Tobago have traveled to Syria to fight with ISIS and other extremist groups against the Syrian Government. Those returning after fighting in Syria will have gained combat skills and would have been further radicalized. It is also common knowledge that Hezbollah has an active presence throughout South America and has operatives in Venezuela. Hezbollah's interests in Latin America are business oriented at this point; they are reportedly involved in money laundering, drug trafficking, and the gold business.

Other sources of potential terrorists are deportees from the United States who have been radicalized in the US prison systems and those who have arrived legally or illegally from such war zones as Syria, Iraq or Libya, etc. The issue with those traveling from troubled countries such as Syria or even Haiti is that it is extremely difficult to confirm their real identities and in locations where there are communities from their own countries potential terrorists and criminals can receive assistance when applying for visas, especially in locations with high government corruption.

With the availability of black-market firearms, porous borders, the abundance of poorly secured tourist resorts and the known presence of terrorist sympathizers we predict it is only a matter of time before there is a notable terrorist incident within the Caribbean.

Maritime Piracy

Incidents of maritime piracy are on the rise in the Southern Caribbean due to the situation in Venezuela. Throughout the Caribbean incidents of small scale, petty thefts and robberies on maritime vessels are not unusual; incidents of assaults and murders happen occasionally but are not common at this point.

The potential for an increase in incidents of maritime piracy, especially targeting private yachts and smaller commercial vessels, is high due to the expansion and influences of the well-armed and organized criminal groups from Venezuela.

On a larger scale, the abundance of commercial vessels such as oil tankers and tourist cruise ships would make easy targets for terrorists. The oil tankers are floating bombs that if attacked and sank would wreak havoc on the Caribbean ecosystem. The unsecured cruise ships are hostage situations waiting to happen.

Money Laundering

Money laundering has always been an issue within the Caribbean but is also an important source of income for many of the islands. Illicit funds are laundered through a variety of methods including the purchase of real estate, vehicles, maritime vessels, and jewelry as well as through an array of legitimate businesses.

The Citizenship by Investment Program (CIP) has been regarded as a major gateway for money laundering and other criminal activities. Many of the sovereign island nations within the Caribbean offer the CIP, and questions have been raised about it allowing known criminals to obtain new identities. This is easily accomplished, especially with those originally from countries that use non-Roman alphabets or from cultures where it is common for a person to have multiple given names and surnames.

The United States has named all major Caribbean countries as Major Money Laundering Jurisdictions* for the year 2018. The only countries left off the list were the US Virgin Islands and Puerto Rico, both US protectorates, along with Martinique and Guadeloupe both of them overseas protectorates of France. Even though these countries may not be on the "Major Money Laundering Jurisdictions" they all suffer from the same permeable borders and trafficking issues as the rest of the Caribbean. Interestingly enough, the European Commission placed the US territories of Puerto Rico, Guam, American Samoa and US Virgin Islands on their Money Laundering Blacklist*. The Caribbean countries on the list are:

• **Antigua and Barbuda:** Money laundering, narcotics trafficking, gaming, and firearms trafficking are major sources of illicit funds in Antigua and Barbuda. The US State Department accused the country's Citizenship By Investment Program (CIP), of being" among the most lax in the world."

• **Aruba:** Aruba is a transshipment point for drugs from South America heading for the United States and Europe, and for currency returning back to South America.

• **Bahamas:** The US claims the major sources of laundered proceeds in the Bahamas are from drug and firearms trafficking, gaming, and human smuggling. Researchers added that drug traffickers and criminal organizations exploit the large number of IBCs and offshore banks registered in the Bahamas to launder money, despite transaction reporting requirements.

• **Barbados:** Drug trafficking, money laundering, and firearms trafficking are major sources of illicit funds in Barbados.

• **British Virgin Islands:** The potential misuse of BVI corporate vehicles remains a concern as money laundered in the BVI predominantly comes from domestic criminal activity and drug trafficking.

• **Cayman Islands:** Most of the money laundering in the Cayman Islands comes from foreign criminal activity such as fraud, tax evasion, and drug trafficking.

• **Cuba:** A known opponent of the US, Cuba was put on the list not because of money laundering but because of its location between drug supplying and drug consuming countries and its lack of cooperation with the U.S.

• **Curaçao:** The primary source of money laundered in Curacao is related to proceeds from illegal narcotics.

• **Dominica:** Money laundered in Dominica comes from foreign fraudulent investment schemes, advance fee fraud schemes, and narcotics activities. The country's Citizenship by Investment Program was also mentioned in the report as being vulnerable to corruption.

• **Dominican Republic:** The major sources of money laundered in the Dominican Republic are illicit trafficking activities, tax evasion, and fraud. The presence of international illicit trafficking cartels, a large informal economy, and weak banking controls make the country appealing for money laundering activities.

• **Grenada:** Money laundering in Grenada is connected to smuggling and drug trafficking by local organized crime groups.

• **Guyana:** The primary sources of laundered funds in Guyana are from narcotics trafficking, corruption, human trafficking, contraband, illegal natural resource extraction, and tax evasion.

- **Haiti:** Money laundered in Haiti comes from drug trafficking, corruption, embezzlement of government funds, smuggling, counterfeiting, kidnappings for ransom, illegal emigration and tax fraud.

- **Jamaica:** Money laundering in Jamaica deals primarily with the proceeds from illegal drugs, financial scams, extortion, financial crimes related to cybercrime, advance fee fraud (lottery scams) and is largely controlled by organized criminal groups.

- **Sint Maarten:** Money laundering in Sint Maarten centers around business investments and its statutes as an international tax shelter.

- **St. Kitts and Nevis:** These Islands have unusually strong bank secrecy laws which inhibit investigations into money laundering and are also at the center of main drug trafficking routes. The country's Citizenship by Investment Program has been "afflicted by significant deficiencies in vetting candidates and conducting due diligence on passport and citizenship recipients after they receive citizenship", claims the U.S.

- **St. Lucia:** The U.S. State Department report states that "Illicit drug trafficking by organized crime rings and the laundering of drug proceeds by domestic and foreign criminal elements remain serious problems for St. Lucia. It is believed financial institutions unwittingly engage in currency transactions involving international narcotics trafficking proceeds".

- **St. Vincent and the Grenadines:** Money laundering and other financial crimes stemming from drug trafficking and its fluid and secretive offshore financial sector. The U.S. State Department report said "The set of islands remains a small but active offshore financial center with a relatively large number of IBCs. United States currency is often smuggled into the country via couriers, go-fast vessels, and yachts".

- **Suriname:** Money laundering is closely linked to transnational criminal activity related to the transshipment of cocaine, which is invested locally in real estate, gold & minerals, foreign exchange companies, casinos, car dealerships, and the construction sector.

• **Trinidad and Tobago:** Drug trafficking, illegal arms sales, fraud, tax evasion, and public corruption are the main sources of illegal cash in Trinidad and Tobago. The State Department report says "Narcotics trafficking organizations and organized crime entities operating locally and internationally, control the majority of illicit proceeds moving through the country".

*U.S. State Department Major Money Laundering Jurisdictions: https://www.state.gov/2019-international-narcotics-control-strategy-report/

*European commission money laundering blacklist: http://europa.eu/rapid/press-release_IP-19-781_en.htm

Corruption

The corruption of law enforcement, government officials and politicians are an international issue of which no country is exempt. The Caribbean cultures harbor over-familiarity and favoritism, and this is a big problem that can be exploited by criminals. Gone are the days when communities were small, and people could be trusted just because they were well known. Criminals seek out and try to align themselves with those who are favored within communities thus giving them legitimacy and helping them to avoid scrutiny.

As we can see from places like current day Mexico, the drug cartels have the money to buy the influence of law enforcement, government officials and politicians at all levels. The Mexican drug cartels are active within Venezuela and no-doubt the Venezuelan criminals are learning their methods of operation. With the expansion of the Venezuelan criminals, we can expect to see a rise in corruption at all levels as well as a rise in violent crimes.

Organized Crime

All the issues we have listed will have direct links to organized crime groups. What we have not mentioned are the additional crimes such as extortion, kidnapping and murder that can be expected wherever criminal groups are operating.

What most people do not understand is that these days most successful crime groups are international organizations that are run to some extent like any other businesses. Their goals are to expand and make money, but unlike a corporation, organized crime groups operate with zero regulations, taxes and virtually total freedom of operations. Their only threats and competition are other criminal groups and effective law enforcement units.

Wars between criminal groups over trafficking routes or territory usually lead to local economies crashing as it's no longer safe for a legitimate business to operate. If such gang wars broke out in the Caribbean this would also greatly affect the tourism industry that many island economies are dependent on.

I stated the other threat to organized criminal groups is effective law enforcement units. By effective we mean well trained and equipped units that have the political backing to be able to combat well-armed and organized criminal groups effectively, without being persecuted themselves by politicians and officials who have been corrupted by the criminal groups they are targeting.

The Caribbean also has an asset that the criminal groups are looking for, a large population of unemployed and restless youths seeking to better themselves. These young men and women are the foot soldiers required by the criminal groups to spread their influence and facilitate their crimes.

Effects Of The Venezuelan Crisis

Venezuela and its communist partner Cuba still have a lot of influence and support within the Caribbean after many years of sanctions and crisis. Venezuela's PetroCaribe oil initiative was set up in 2005 to provide cheap oil to Caribbean member countries and as a way of spreading Venezuelan influence through the region. PetroCaribe currently has 17 members including Antigua and Barbuda, the Bahamas, Belize, Cuba, Dominica, the Dominican Republic, Grenada, Guyana, Haiti, Jamaica, St Lucia, St Kitts and Nevis, St Vincent and the Grenadines, and Suriname. Since the crisis in Venezuela, the PetroCaribe oil initiative continues but at a much-reduced level compared to what it was operating at before.

Throughout the Caribbean, the Cuban and Venezuelan governments supply doctors and nurses to many of the Islands. There is a lack of trained doctors and nurses throughout the Caribbean, as many locals after they receive the relevant schooling and certification immigrate to such locations as the United Kingdom where the pay and conditions are far better than in their own countries. The Cuban and Venezuelan medical staff make up for the shortage of trained locals.

Venezuela has become a hub location for cocaine coming out of South America and heading for the US, Europe, and Africa via air and sea routes. The Mexican drug cartels have representatives in Venezuela to broker drug deals with the local drug gangs that are controlled by the Venezuelan military and intelligence services. Organized crime groups including Hezbollah are actively involved in Venezuela's gold mining operations and trafficking. In addition to a marketplace, Venezuela offers a safe haven for international criminals and terrorists.

To survive in today's Venezuela most people have to be corrupted or working with criminal groups to some extent. UNHCR reported in June 2019 that 4 million Venezuelans have chosen to flee the country and in their midst are hardened criminals and murderers seeking opportunities to ply their trade in other countries. For those in the criminal groups, the crisis in Venezuela is proving to be lucrative as they can operate with impunity as long as they are well aligned and pay the required tributes when called for.

As the crisis in Venezuela continues and their criminal economy becomes one of the country's main sources of income its criminal gangs will become more sophisticated and start to seek out new territories and alliances within the region and internationally.

At this time the Venezuelan criminals are active in the Caribbean, trafficking people, firearms and drugs. In the future, as they seek to control territory throughout the region, they will become active in extortion, kidnapping, violent crimes and murder.

The United States

Whether the United States is a positive or negative influence on the Caribbean is a matter of opinion, especially after their recent fiasco of attempted regime change in Venezuela.

Most of the Caribbean islands were and to some extent, still are, heavily influenced by European laws and culture, which are very different from the laws and culture of the United States. Most of the Caribbean, outside of the tourist resorts, is very conservative and let's say hold traditional values. The United States usually forgets such things and believes everyone should see things from their perspective.

It is common knowledge that the majority of illegal drugs passing through the Caribbean are destined for the United States and the majority of the guns and ammunition coming into the Caribbean is coming from the United States.

The United States economy is dependent on the proceeds from illegal drugs, so we must ask the question, do they really want to eradicate drug trafficking? If you take illegal narcotics out of the US economy then how many jobs will be lost for police officers, prison staff, lawyers and rehab workers on the surface, and how would this, in turn, affect the US economy? The US's drug addiction even motivated family doctors and pharmaceutical companies to get in on the market, that's why the US is now suffering a major opioid epidemic. So, whose interest are they focusing on in their foreign and drug policies, those of a poor Caribbean Island or their own?

Another issue that is causing problems is that of the deportees that are being sent back from the United States after being convicted or serving prison sentences. The United States has the right to deport these criminals, many of whom were in the country illegally, but the issues arise when they return to their countries of origin. These people bring with them the advanced criminal skill sets they learned in the United States and also a network of international contacts.

One strange action by the United States was the sanctioning of the security forces and police of Saint Lucia under the Leahy Laws for human rights violations. Countries under sanctions from Leahy Laws are unable to receive U.S. military or police assistance, training and arms, etc. In 2013, Saint Lucia was sanctioned under the Leahy Laws due to what were believed to be 17 extrajudicial killings of known criminals. When you look at the statistics of people killed in the United States by police officers annually, especially those who were unarmed or mentally ill, I am very sure the number would far exceed that of those who are killed by police officers in the entire Caribbean.

As we said at the start of this chapter, whether the United States is a positive or negative influence on the Caribbean is a matter of opinion.

COUNTRY PROFILES

Antigua And Barbuda

· **Population:** 95,882 (July 2018 est.)

· **GDP - per capita (PPP):** $26,400 (2017 est.)

· **Industries:** Tourism, construction, light manufacturing (clothing, alcohol, household appliances)

· **Exports:** Petroleum products, bedding, handicrafts, electronic components, transport equipment, food, and live animals

· **Imports:** Food and live animals, machinery and transport equipment, manufactures, chemicals, oil

Tourism dominates Antigua and Barbuda's economy, accounting for nearly 60% of GDP and 40% of the investment. Antigua and Barbuda's has an established offshore financial industry that has come under scrutiny for money laundering. Antigua and Barbuda is reported to have a problem with human trafficking, specifically the trafficking of women from the Dominican Republic, Haiti, Jamaica and Guyana who are trafficked to work either in the few illegal brothels or forced into involuntary domestic service in private homes. Like most of the Islands in the area, Antigua and Barbuda has a problem with being a transit location for international drug trafficking. While there is petty crime in Antigua and Barbuda the overall crime rates are very low.

Bahamas

· **Population:** 332,634 (July 2018 est.)

· **GDP - per capita (PPP):** $32,400 (2017 est.)

• **Industries:** Tourism, banking, oil bunkering, maritime industries, transshipment and logistics, salt, aragonite, pharmaceuticals

• **Exports:** Rock lobster, aragonite, crude salt, polystyrene products

• **Imports:** Machinery and transport equipment, manufactures, chemicals, mineral fuels; food and live animals

Tourism provides approximately 50% of the Bahamas GDP and is the main source of employment for 50% of the country's workforce. The Bahamian financial services sector is the country's second-most important sector of the economy and provides 15% of GDP. The U.S. State Department reports the Bahamian financial services sector has been exploited by criminal gangs for money laundering. Due to its proximity to the United States, the Bahamas is a transit location for humans and drugs being trafficked into the U.S. and for illegal firearms and ammunition being trafficked out of the US and into the Caribbean. Violent crimes and sexual assaults against tourists are common and are an issue where the Government is making progress, but visitors are still advised to be very careful.

Barbados

• **Population:** 293,131 (July 2018 est.)

• **GDP - per capita (PPP):** $18,600 (2017 est.)

• **Industries:** Tourism, sugar, light manufacturing, component assembly for export

• **Exports:** Manufactures, sugar, molasses, rum, other foodstuffs and beverages, chemicals, electrical components

• **Imports:** Consumer goods, machinery, foodstuffs, construction materials, chemicals, fuel, electrical components

Tourism is the leading sector in the Barbados economy, accounting for 12% of GDP, it's indirect contribution to GDP is an estimated 40% and is also the largest source of jobs. Barbados is a major drugs hub for marijuana and cocaine for distribution and sale within the Caribbean or to be trafficked further afield into the U.S. and Europe. The illegal drugs arrive in Barbados by various means including fast boats, couriers, airdrops from Venezuela, Guyana and other Islands within the Caribbean. Serious crime and violence rates are low in Barbados.

Cuba

- **Population:** 11,116,396 (July 2018 est.)
- **GDP - per capita (PPP):** $12,300 (2016 est.)
- **Industries:** Petroleum, nickel, cobalt, pharmaceuticals, tobacco, construction, steel, cement, agricultural machinery, sugar
- **Exports:** Petroleum, nickel, medical products, sugar, tobacco, fish, citrus, coffee
- **Imports:** Petroleum, food, machinery and equipment, chemicals

The Communist Cuban government is nearly bankrupt and economically inefficient. Most jobs are low-productivity functions in Cuba's government sector. In Cuba there is political interference in all aspects of life, private property is strictly regulated, excessive bureaucracy limits trade and any possible investments. There are virtually no statistics on crime or trafficking in Cuba but due to its geographical location, government corruption and close ties with Venezuela we can take it for granted government officials are directly or indirectly involved in human and drug trafficking. Video has recently surfaced on social media of a Cuban mercenary who was working with pro-government militias in Bolivar State, Venezuela who was captured by a rival criminal gang involved in the gold business and smuggling, etc.

The Commonwealth Of Dominica

- **Population:** 74,027 (July 2018 est.)

- **GDP - per capita (PPP):** $11,000 (2017 est.)

- **Industries:** Soap, coconut oil, tourism, copra, furniture, cement blocks, shoes

- **Exports:** Bananas, soap, bay oil, vegetables, grapefruit, oranges

- **Imports:** Manufactured goods, machinery, and equipment, food, chemicals

Dominica has become a major international financial hub and its offshore services are its main source of income. There has been an international concern that Dominica's offshore services are facilitating money laundering for criminal groups and its Citizenship by Investment Program has been condemned as being very vulnerable to corruption. Dominica has suffered from economic issues over the last few years and like other islands in the area is a transit point for drug traffickers. There were reports that after Hurricane Maria in 2017, armed drug gangs were openly patrolling and looting the capital, Roseau.

Dominican Republic

- **Population:** 10,298,756 (July 2018 est.)

- **GDP - per capita (PPP):** $17,000 (2017 est.)

- **Industries:** Tourism, sugar processing, gold mining, textiles, cement, tobacco, electrical components, medical devices

- **Exports:** Gold, silver, cocoa, sugar, coffee, tobacco, meats, consumer goods

- **Imports:** Petroleum, foodstuffs, cotton and fabrics, chemicals and pharmaceuticals

The Dominican Republic (DR) has one of the fastest growing economies in the region and has a reputation for corruption at all levels. Luxury property investments in the DR are one of the main covers for Money Laundering, the country is also a hub for drugs, arms, and human trafficking. Organized crime and drug trafficking groups are active in the Dominican Republic and engaged in a wide variety of criminal activities. Prostitutes from the Dominican Republic can be found throughout the Caribbean, they travel legally or are trafficked illegally to their countries of choice where they set up business with the help of Dominicans already in place.

Guadeloupe (French Territory)

· **Population**: 395,700 (April 2019 est.)

· **GDP - per capita (PPP)**: $25,479 (2014 est.)

The Guadeloupe economy depends on tourism, the export of bananas, sugar, and rum and is largely subsidized by France. Unemployment in Guadeloupe especially among the youth is very high, which is something that can be exploited by criminal groups as a potential recruiting ground. Guadeloupe is a transit point for human, arms and drug trafficking.

Martinique (French Territory)

· **Population:** 376,480 (2016 est.)

· **GDP - per capita (PPP):** US$27,688 (2012 est.)

The Martinique economy depends strongly on tourism as its main source of income and employment. Martinique like other Islands in the area is a transit point for human, arms and drug trafficking. Martinique is reportedly one of the main transit points for drugs heading to Europe.

Saint Barthélemy (French Territory)

· **Population:** 9,625 (2015 est.)

· **GDP - per capita (PPP):** US$37,000 (2007 est.)

Saint Barthélemy has a very high standard of living when compared to other islands in the Caribbean, this is due to its tourism industry that has attracted a lot of international investment and wealthy clientele. Due to its location, Saint Barthélemy is on the drug, arms and human trafficking routes but suffers far less from these issues than other islands because of its flourishing economy.

Saint Martin (French Territory)

• **Population:** 35,107 (2014 est.)

• **GDP - per capita (PPP):** US$20,600 (2007 est.)

French Saint Martin is the northern 60% of the divided Caribbean island of Saint Martin and tourism accounts for 80% of the economy and employment. As with the other Islands in the area, Saint Martin is a transit point for drugs, human and arms trafficking.

Grenada

• **Population:** 112,207 (July 2018 est.)

• **GDP - per capita (PPP):** $1.634 billion (2017 est.)

• **Industries:** Food and beverages, textiles, light assembly operations, tourism, construction, education, call-center operations

• **Exports:** Nutmeg, bananas, cocoa, fruit and vegetables, clothing, mace, chocolate, fish

• **Imports:** Food, manufactured goods, machinery, chemicals, fuel

Grenada's economy is weak when compared with other countries in the region and relies greatly on tourism as a main source of income. Grenada has received criticism for weak oversight of its Citizen by Investment Program which is open to exploitation by criminals due to government corruption etc. As with the other Islands in the region, it is a transit location for traffickers.

Guyana

• **Population:** 740,685 (July 2018 est.)

- **GDP - per capita (PPP):** $8,100 (2017 est.)

- **Industries:** Bauxite, sugar, rice milling, timber, textiles, gold mining

- **Exports:** Sugar, gold, bauxite, alumina, rice, shrimp, molasses, rum, timber

- **Imports:** Manufactures, machinery, petroleum, food

Guyana is one of the fastest developing countries in the Western Hemisphere and also a hub location for trafficking and organized crime. Drugs from South America are trafficked to Guyana and then trafficked by air or sea into the Caribbean and onward to the United States, Europe, and Africa. Gold plays a big part in the local economy and is legally mined within the country. Also illegally mined gold is trafficked in from neighboring countries such as Surinam and Venezuela. Corruption is a major problem within Guyana.

Haiti

- **Population:** 10,788,440 (July 2018 est.)

- **GDP - per capita (PPP):** $1,800 (2017 est.)

- **Industries:** Textiles, sugar refining, flour milling, cement, light assembly using imported parts

- **Exports:** Apparel, manufactures, oils, cocoa, mangoes, coffee

- **Imports:** Food, manufactured goods, machinery, and transport equipment, fuels, raw materials

Haiti is a country that suffers from severe poverty and corruption. Many Haitians seek to flee Haiti by legal travel and being trafficked to other islands in the Caribbean or to the United States. Haiti has been a haven and transit point for drug traffickers for many years with many of the country's leading politicians being connected with the illegal drugs trade. Haiti is also a transit location for firearms and ammunition being trafficked out of the U.S.

Jamaica

- **Population:** 2,812,090 (July 2018 est.)
- **GDP - per capita (PPP):** $9,200 (2017 est.)
- **Industries:** Agriculture, mining, manufacture, construction, financial and insurance services, tourism, telecommunications
- **Exports:** Alumina, bauxite, chemicals, coffee, mineral fuels, waste and scrap metals, sugar, yams
- **Imports:** Food and other consumer goods, industrial supplies, fuel, parts and accessories of capital goods, machinery and transport equipment, construction materials

Tourism is the main source of income and jobs in Jamaica's fragile economy. Jamaica suffers from high unemployment, high crime rates, drug, violence and gang activity.

Aruba (Netherlands Territory)

- **Population:** 116,576 (July 2018 est.)
- **GDP - per capita (PPP):** $37,500 (2017 est.)
- **Industries:** Tourism, petroleum transshipment facilities, banking
- **Exports:** Live animals and animal products, art and collectibles, machinery and electrical equipment, transport equipment
- **Imports:** Machinery and electrical equipment, refined oil for bunkering and reexport, chemicals; foodstuffs

Aruba like many other Caribbean islands relies on tourism as the mainstay of its economy. Due to its location, Aruba is a natural transit point for drugs being trafficked out of South America and drug money being returned. Aruba has a reputation for corruption but in recent years has been working to rectify the issues of the past. The US State Department removed Aruba from the list of major drugs producing and transit countries in 1999...

Curaçao (Netherlands Territory)

• **Population:** 150,241 (July 2018 est.)

• **GDP - per capita (PPP):** $15,000 (2004 est.)

• **Industries:** Tourism, petroleum refining, petroleum transshipment, light manufacturing, financial and business services

• **Exports:** Petroleum products

• **Imports:** Crude petroleum, food, manufactures

Compared to other Islands in the Caribbean, Curacao has a high per capita income and a very good infrastructure. Curacao's main sources of income are tourism, petroleum-related services, and offshore financial services. Due to its location, it is a natural transit point for drug trafficking and the laundering of drug money.

Sint Maarten (Netherlands Territory)

• **Population:** 42,677 (July 2018 est.)

• **GDP - per capita (PPP):** $66,800 (2014 est.)

• **Industries:** Tourism, light industry

The economy in Sint Maarten relies on tourism which employs the majority of the island's workforce. Sint Maarten is the southern 40% of the divided island of Saint Martin and has the 14th largest GDP per capita in the world, which is over three times higher than the French controlled north of the Island. After Hurricane Irma in 2017, there were many cases of tourist resorts being looted by armed gangs and Dutch soldiers were deployed to back up local law enforcement. There has been an international concern that Sint Maarten's offshore financial sector is being used to launder money from drug trafficking and organized crime and like other islands in the area, it is a transit point for drugs being trafficked from South America.

Saint Kitts And Nevis

- **Population:** 53,094 (July 2018 est.)
- **GDP - per capita (PPP):** $28,200 (2017 est.)
- **Industries:** Tourism, cotton, salt, copra, clothing, footwear, beverages
- **Exports:** Machinery, food, electronics, beverages, tobacco
- **Imports:** Machinery, manufactures, food, fuels

Saint Kitts and Nevis like most islands in the Caribbean relies on tourism as its main source of income but has diversified into the offshore financial sectors. Saint Kitts and Nevis Citizenship by Investment Program has drawn criticism because of the thoroughness of its due diligence investigation. Saint Kitts and Nevis have high crime and violence rates which for the most part are reported to be drug crime related, rarely do these crimes affect tourists.

Saint Lucia

- **Population:** 165,510 (July 2018 est.)
- **GDP - per capita (PPP):** $14,400 (2017 est.)
- **Industries:** Tourism; clothing, assembly of electronic components, beverages, corrugated cardboard boxes, lime processing, coconut processing
- **Exports:** Bananas, clothing, cocoa, avocados, mangoes, coconut oil
- **Imports:** Food, manufactured goods, machinery, and transportation equipment, chemicals, fuels

Tourism reportedly accounts for 65% of Saint Lucia's GDP and the island still has a sizable agricultural export sector. Crime rates on Saint Lucia are higher than on neighboring islands, with 60 murders reported in 2017. Robbery can also be a problem and there have been some high-profile incidents but in general, tourists are not often affected. Due to its location, it is a transit point for drugs and human trafficking.

Saint Vincent And The Grenadines

· **Population:** 101,844 (July 2018 est.)

· **GDP - per capita (PPP):** $11,500 (2017 est.)

· **Industries:** Tourism; food processing, cement, furniture, clothing, starch

· **Exports:** Bananas, eddoes, and dasheen (taro), arrowroot starch; tennis racquets

· **Imports:** Foodstuffs, machinery and equipment, chemicals and fertilizers, minerals and fuels

Saint Vincent and the Grenadines economy is dominated by banana production, there are small and developing tourism and offshore financial service sectors. While crime is relatively low the islands are a transit location for cocaine heading north from Venezuela and domestically grown marijuana heading south where it is generally exchanged for cocaine and firearms.

Trinidad And Tobago

· **Population:** 1,215,527 (July 2018 est.)

· **GDP - per capita (PPP):** $31,300 (2017 est.)

· **Industries:** Petroleum and petroleum products, liquefied natural gas, methanol, ammonia, urea, steel products, beverages, food processing, cement, cotton textiles

· **Exports:** Petroleum and petroleum products, liquefied natural gas, methanol, ammonia, urea, steel products, beverages, cereal and cereal products, cocoa, fish, preserved fruits, cosmetics, household cleaners, plastic packaging

• **Imports:** Mineral fuels, lubricants, machinery, transportation equipment, manufactured goods, food, chemicals, live animals

Oil and gas account for about 40% of Trinidad and Tobago's GDP and 80% of exports but employs less than 5% of the workforce. Citizens from Trinidad and Tobago have traveled to Syria where they have fought with Islamic Extremist organizations such as ISIS which raises fears of the threat of Islamic Extremist activity within the region. Trinidad and Tobago has high crime rates and its proximity to Venezuela has led to an increase in drug, arms and human trafficking. Venezuelan maritime pirates have been targeting fishing boats and small commercial vessels in waters around Trinidad and Tobago.

Anguilla (United Kingdom Territory)

• **Population:** 17,422 (July 2018 est.)

• **GDP - per capita (PPP):** $12,200 (2008 est.)

• **Industries:** Tourism, boat building, offshore financial services

• **Exports:** Lobster, fish, livestock, salt, concrete blocks, rum

• **Imports:** Fuels, foodstuffs, manufactures, chemicals, trucks, textiles

Anguilla is a small Island that relies on luxury travel and offshore banking and financial services. Prostitution is legal in Anguilla and in the last few years has seen an influx of sex workers from the Dominican Republic and Venezuela.

British Virgin Islands (United Kingdom Territory)

• **Population:** 35,802 (July 2018 est.)

• **GDP - per capita (PPP):** $34,200 (2017 est.)

• **Industries:** Tourism, light industry, construction, rum, concrete block, offshore banking center

· **Exports:** Rum, fresh fish, fruits, animals; gravel, sand

· **Imports:** Building materials, automobiles, foodstuffs, machinery

Tourism is the main source of income for the British Virgin Islands (BVI) which accounts for 45% of its GDP. The BVI also has an offshore financial sector that has strict confidentiality laws that undoubtedly has attracted dirty money that is being laundered on behalf of criminal organizations. Due to its location, BVI is a transit point for drug trafficking and due to its flourishing tourist industry is a destination for prostitutes seeking wealthy clients.

Cayman Islands (United Kingdom Territory)

· **Population:** 59,613 (July 2018 est.)

· **GDP - per capita (PPP):** $43,800 (2004 est.)

· **Industries:** Tourism, banking, insurance and finance, construction, construction materials, furniture

· **Exports:** Turtle products, manufactured consumer goods

· **Imports:** Foodstuffs, manufactured goods, fuels

Luxury Tourism accounts for about 70% of the Cayman Islands GDP it also has a well-established offshore banking and financial sector. Crime rates in the Cayman Islands have risen over the past few years but it is still a very safe location for visitors. Money laundering is a major problem for the Cayman Islands but in reality, is one of the main reasons for their thriving offshore financial sector.

Montserrat (United Kingdom Territory)

· **Population:** 5,315 (July 2018 est.)

· **GDP - per capita (PPP):** $34,000 (2011 est.)

· **Industries:** Tourism, rum, textiles, electronic appliances

• **Exports:** Electronic components, plastic bags, apparel; hot peppers, limes, live plants; cattle

• **Imports:** Machinery and transportation equipment, foodstuffs, manufactured goods, fuels, lubricants

Between 1995 and 2000, two-thirds of Montserrat's population was forced to flee due to volcanic eruptions. Montserrat has a limited economy and is largely supported by the British Government. There have been incidents of drug traffickers and marijuana growers using the section of the island that is still a no-go zone due to volcanic activity.

Turks And Caicos Islands (United Kingdom Territory)

• **Population:** 53,701 (July 2018 est.)

• **GDP - per capita (PPP):** $29,100 (2007 est.)

• **Industries:** Tourism, offshore financial services

• **Exports:** Lobster, dried and fresh conch, conch shells

• **Imports:** Food and beverages, tobacco, clothing, manufactures, construction materials

The economy of the Turks and Caicos Islands is based on tourism, offshore financial services, and fishing. The Turks and Caicos suffer from problems with illegal immigrants being trafficked from Haiti who also bring drugs and firearms with them. Violent crime is common in the Turks and Caicos and tourists have been actively targeted, this issue is played down by the government for the sake of the tourism sector.

Puerto Rico (United States Territory)

• **Population:** 3,294,626 (July 2018 est.)

• **GDP - per capita (PPP):** $39,400 (2017 est.)

- **Industries:** Pharmaceuticals, electronics, apparel, food products, tourism

- **Exports:** Chemicals, electronics, apparel, canned tuna, rum, beverage concentrates, medical equipment

- **Imports:** Chemicals, machinery, and equipment, clothing, food, fish, petroleum products

Puerto Rico's economy has been in trouble for many years mainly due to government corruption. In addition to its economic problems, drug, gang and violent crime rates are high. Even though it is a US territory it is a transit location and marketplace for drugs, firearms and human trafficking.

United States Virgin Islands (United States Territory)

- **Population:** 106,977 (July 2018 est.)

- **GDP - per capita (PPP):** $37,000 (2016 est.)

- **Industries:** Tourism, watch assembly, rum distilling, construction, pharmaceuticals, electronics

- **Exports:** Rum

- **Imports:** Foodstuffs, consumer goods, building materials

Tourism is the mainstay of the economy in the United States Virgin Islands as with many other of the islands in the Caribbean. In 2018 the United States Virgin Islands had the highest murder rate in the Caribbean with 52 people killed. The United States Virgin Islands are a transit location for cocaine heading North from South America into the US and for firearms from the US heading in the Caribbean.

Conclusion

As you can see from the previous chapters the Caribbean economy relies heavily on tourism and in a part of the world that is prone to natural disasters and hurricanes. We also mentioned the huge potential for terrorist attacks against tourist targets. Major incidents affecting the tourism industry within the Caribbean could devastate local economies and destabilize the region.

Areas where there is high unemployment, corruption and struggling economies are always vulnerable to organized crime. People need to eat and feed their families and when they cannot do so by legitimate means they will turn to crime. Within the Caribbean, they would not have to look far as the drug trade is booming due to the United States and Europe's insatiable appetites.

Such is the situation in Venezuela where organized crime, drug and gold trafficking, etc. are becoming mainstays of the economy. Be assured the criminal and trafficking organizations within Venezuela are seeking to expand their operations and struggling economies within the Caribbean are definitely in their sights.

Some of the islands have diversified their economies with offshore banking and financial services which has drawn criticism for facilitating money laundering. But what are their alternatives, growing sugar cane and making rum? People need to make money and what some may see as criminal is what others have to do to survive.

The issues with the vast majority of those criticizing and giving opinions on what is best for the Caribbean is that they have little or no understanding of the countries, the cultures and the ordinary people's lives other than what they have seen on PowerPoint presentations, or while being driven around in official vehicles and staying in five-star accommodation. What's best for the Caribbean can only be decided by those who originate from the islands and live there.

Top of the list of recommendations for the future stability of the Caribbean is that the region needs to find stable and sustainable industries on which to base their economies. As I am definitely not an expert in the economic development field all we will say on this matter is that if economies struggle and fail then the criminals quickly exploit the situation as they have in Venezuela.

My recommendations for what is needed to enhance the security of the region are below. They are an obvious recommendation for anyone who has an understanding of the situation.

Effective Intelligence Gathering & Sharing

The basis of successful security programs is knowing the threats you need to counter, and this begins with good intelligence. Once intelligence has been accurately gathered on criminals, their gangs, their networks, methods of operations and trafficking routes, etc. it needs to be shared with the relevant law enforcement organizations and units locally and within the region. In simple terms, effective intelligence gathering, and sharing will mean the criminals can be successfully identified, located and targeted.

Surveillance

Every island in the Caribbean has a problem with porous borders and an abundance of isolated beaches and landing spots for fishing or fast boats and yachts. These days there is an abundance of surveillance equipment and drones available that could be tactically employed to detect illegal inshore activity and landings.

Detection

Detection methods for drugs, firearms, and cash at ports, international points of entry and areas of known criminal activity needs to be enhanced. There is a severe lack of properly trained sniffer dogs, search equipment and training throughout the Caribbean.

Security Force & Police Training

Local security forces and police need to receive relevant training for the environments that they work in and the types of crime they will be dealing with. A lot of the law enforcement training in the Caribbean is provided by agencies from the United States. This is OK but the laws and environment within the Caribbean are completely different from what you would find in the United States. The emphasis seems to be put on tactical training, use of force and human rights training where the real need is for intelligence, undercover operations, and surveillance training. When looking at the potential threats for the near future such as the criminal gangs coming out of Venezuela they need to be viewed in the context of a counterinsurgency. This might sound extreme but all you have to do is look at the situations in Mexico and Venezuela to see that the threat from trained, experienced and well-armed organized criminal groups is very real.

Community Security

Communities need to be protected and confident that the authorities are working in their interests before they will fully cooperate and assist security forces and police. Sadly, organized criminal groups seem to understand this better than most security forces and police agencies and effectively use local communities to work in their favor. Effectively interacting, educating, gaining the confidence of, and working with local communities is essential in combating the threat of organized crime.

Caribbean Based Response

In conclusion, to combat the potential threats facing the countries and territories of the Caribbean there need to be effective proactive measures that specifically address and tackle the potential threats while understanding the local cultures and taking into consideration the needs of the local communities.

APPENDIX 1: THE
VENEZUELA THREAT

For many people, the situation in Venezuela is just another political arguing point that has recently been in the news due to President Trump's recognition of the country's political opposition leader Juan Guaidó as interim president as a result of the failing communist government of Nicolás Maduro.

What most people do not understand and what is not being mentioned in the media is that Venezuela is very much a "Narco" state. As well as being a country that is rich in oil and other natural resources it is also a hub for drugs being trafficked from South America into the U.S. and Europe via the Caribbean.

Many parts of the country are controlled by narco-traffickers who work hand in hand with the Venezuelan police and national guard to facilitate the secure transportation of narcotics to and from airstrips, or from the airstrips to fast boats on the Caribbean coast.

In addition to the narco gangs, Venezuela also has a long-established terrorist connection with groups such as Hezbollah who has a presence in the country. In 2016 Abu Wa'el Dhiab, one of six people released from US military detention in Guantanamo Bay resettled in Uruguay and consequently turned up in Caracas, the Venezuelan capital, it's still not clear how he got there.

Hezbollah is known to have a presence in other parts of South America, especially in the tri-border area where Argentina, Paraguay, and Brazil converge. In 2018 a Hezbollah 'Treasurer" Assad Ahmad Barakat was arrested for laundering $10 million USD through various casinos in the Iguazu Falls area of the Brazilian state of Paraná. The group's presence in South America is ingrained in the cocaine and money laundering business.

For the innocent people reading let me explain something that should be clear after reading the above few paragraphs. Drug traffickers, organized crime groups and terrorists all work together whether trafficking drugs, arms, laundering money, kidnapping, extorting or assassinations. They are a combined threat, with extremely efficient communications, intelligence, logistics, and operational networks.

At this time Venezuela is proving to be a safe haven for both narcos and terrorists alike, so if you think what you are seeing in the news reports is just more political charades then I hope this article will open your eyes to the real situation and how it can destabilize the entire region.

The Main Narco Cartels Operating In Venezuela

Below I have listed the main named cartels operating in Venezuela, but you must remember that just like Mexico and other such places there are many local gangs and organized crime groups that operate with these cartels when mutually profitable but also run their own operations. Even if the heads of the large narco-trafficking groups are eliminated or arrested the operations will continue as the actual ground operations are being conducted by numerous semi-independent trafficking and organized crime groups. You are not dealing with a static business structure but rather a fluid and ever-evolving network.

• **Cartel de Los Soles:** Run by high ranking Venezuelan military officers and top politicians. Diosdado Cabello (Head of the cartel and president of the official Bolivarian party - PSUV), Néstor Reverol (minister of internal affairs and justice), Padrino López (minister of defense). All of them close to Presidente Maduro. This cartel was established over two decades ago by providing security to the Colombian and Mexican cartels. Since 2005 they took over the business and now not even a kilo of pure Colombian cocaine gets to Venezuela without their knowledge. The Venezuelan Army, Navy, Air Force, and National Guard are all involved.

• **ELN (Ejército de Liberación Nacional):** The Colombian guerrilla group is the main drug supplier, they control most of the Venezuelan and Colombian border and are causing chaos in Táchira and Zulia States. Since 2018 the ELN has also gotten involved in the gold business in Bolivar state which borders Brazil. Since the Colombian guerrilla group, the FARC, have officially disbanded the ELN has taken over, they can be classed as the "New kids on the block" and are operating with the Venezuelan government's blessing and assistance.

• **Hezbollah:** With many years of operating in Venezuela this terrorist organization has major links to the Venezuelan government, allies and business associates. Their operations in Venezuela include drug trafficking, arms dealing, terrorist training, money laundering and involvement in gold mining operations. Hezbollah facilitators and operators are spread across Venezuela, but their headquarters are on Margarita Island in the South Caribbean. Tareck El Aissami who has a reputation for being a "strong man" of the Venezuelan communist government and is a former government official is responsible for the Hezbollah in Venezuela. President Nicolás Maduro appointed El Aissami as Vice-President in 2017, which also made him head of Venezuela's intelligence agency (SEBIN). El Aissami has faced allegations of corruption, money laundering, drug trafficking, human rights violations and being linked to terrorist organizations from the U.S. and others. El Aissami is currently under sanctions from Canada, the European Union, Switzerland, and the United States. It's reported that members of El Aissami's family, including his father and mother, relocated to the United States in 2016.

• **Pranes:** This is a domestic organized crime group that is controlled by and recruits from those in the Venezuelan prison system. They are very well-armed, and its main business is extortion, murder, kidnapping and they also provide security and services to some of the cartels. They are connected to and protected by the government as they do a lot of dirty work for them and the narcos.

· **Venezuelan Police, Military and National Security Services:** State Police, National Police, and military services are involved in facilitating the drug business. The CICPC (Investigation Police) and SEBIN (National Bolivarian Intelligence Service) are the ones "babysitting" narcos, terrorist and criminals within Venezuela and are also active sellers of drugs for the domestic drugs market.

Trafficking Routes

The traffickers bringing drugs and weapon in and out of Venezuela use both land, air, and sea routes. Due to the corruption within the police and military, the traffickers can easily get through any border checkpoints or roadblocks they may encounter within the country. Large government sanctioned shipments are moved in military or police vehicles.

Small planes use isolated or rural airstrips to bring shipments into Venezuela and North into the Caribbean. In addition to using disused government airstrips traffickers cut and resurface their own strips in areas that are convenient for their operation. In areas completely under their control hard surfaced roads are used as airstrips. During these landing operations, the roads are closed to traffic by the local police and military.

· **Falcón State:** From villages such as Tucacas, Chichiriviche, La Vela and Puerto Cumarebo, narcos are deploying speed boats to transport drugs into Aruba, Curaçao and Dominican Republic. Since the local farmers have abandoned their lands the narcos and their associates are buying or simply just using the abandoned farmland to cut airstrips and facilitate their operations. The U.S. is well aware of the large number of narco-flights that take off from Venezuela during the night. It is reported and believable that Law Enforcement agencies in the Islands of Aruba and Curaçao, which are very close to Venezuela are infiltrated and corrupted by the Venezuelan narcos. It should be noted the embarkation points for narco boats from Tucacas and La Vela de Coro are right next to National Guard and Coast Guard posts.

• **Zulia State:** Next to Colombia, Zulia State is the most violent state in Venezuela and is a hub location for narco flights heading for such places as Honduras, Panamá and Dominican Republic. The Mexican drug cartels are established and operating from the State's main city, Maracaibo.

• **Apure State:** This is one of the poorest states within Venezuela and borders Colombia. Apure State is dominated by the Venezuelan FBL and Colombian ELN guerrillas that organize and facilitate the narco-trafficking. It's reported the State has over 100 operational narco airstrips at any given time.

• **Sucre State:** Local fisherman have found that the drug business, and now piracy, is a profitable way of making easy money. Villages such as San Juan de Gandoles, Güiria and Carupano are under the domain of the Venezuelan organized crime groups, Pranes, and the Cartel de Los Soles. In San Juan de las Galdonas it's reported by local sources there are approximately 400 narcos who are in possession of heavy weapons. In addition to airstrips in the area, drugs are brought in from the Colombian border by military trucks to be transported by fast boats into the Caribbean. The state has a strategic location as it is close to Trinidad and Tobago and only a few days by boat from Puerto Rico. Recently it has turned into a war zone as the local gangs are fighting for control and also branching out into maritime piracy. The corruption in Sucre State also spreads into Trinidad and Tobago, as everyone eats from the narcos' table...

The regular Venezuelan citizens living in the rural and narco controlled areas are at the mercy of the criminals and corrupt police. It is very much a case of "Plata o Plomo" or in English "Silver or Lead". They have no choice but to look the other way, do as they are told and help the narcos if requested if they want to ensure their safety and that of their families.

In addition to the active threats I have spoken about so far, I will also mention two more potential threats:

· **Maritime Piracy:** In the waters between Venezuela and Trinidad and Tobago there have been numerous hijackings and kidnappings of local fishermen. In April 2018, 15 Guyanese fishermen were killed when their boats were attacked off the Suriname coast. With the collapse and corruption of Law Enforcement within Venezuela and the ineffectiveness of the Law Enforcement agencies in the other Southern Caribbean Islands, the pirates can roam free. If we are being honest about things as long as they are only attacking local fishermen no-one really cares but it's only a matter of time if you ask me before they attack or hijack a yacht or other more valuable vessels than local fishing boats.

· **Terrorism:** As I stated earlier Hezbollah has an established presence in Venezuela and there have been reports of ISIS members in the country. Trinidad and Tobago also has an issue with Islamic extremism and many of its citizens have fought with ISIS in Syria, so we can safely say there is a potential Islamic extremist threat in the Southern Caribbean. Combine the presence of potential terrorists with the availability of military grade weapons on the black market and covert transportation routes into the U.S. and Europe and I think unless you're completely stupid you will see there is a big problem waiting to happen. But the terrorists would not need to go too far to find some very soft targets in the Southern Caribbean such as the oil platforms around Trinidad and Tobago or even better, one of the many unprotected cruise ships ferrying tourists from tropical island to tropical island. I am sure you get the picture, so it's pointless for me to mention all the unprotected tourist resorts and hotels dotted across the islands where tourists are lounging around swimming pools waiting to be kidnapped, etc...

Venezuela is a failed State, but can things be put back in order? Well, anything can be fixed if people want it to be fixed. The issue with Venezuela is that so many people are making money from those situations not being fixed including the supposed political opposition. In Miami it's common knowledge that a lot of very wealthy Venezuelans are buying properties and businesses, but where is their money coming from? How many of the supposed political opposition are still doing business with the Venezuelan government and how much of their dirty money is being laundered in Miami's new luxury condo buildings etc.?

Even though in 2018 the U.S. government claimed it was clamping down on dirty cash being used for property deals in Miami and other such places, the reality is that the money keeps flowing, and in Miami you don't even have to mention "lead" for people just to take your money with a smile...

APPENDIX 2: WAR IN VENEZUELA

On the morning of April 30th, 2019 Venezuela's opposition leader Juan Guaidó seemed to attempt a coup d'état against the communist government of Nicolás Maduro. I use the word seemed because it can be best described as a publicity stunt more than an actual coup d'état. For the remainder of the day, even those that thought they knew what was going on in Venezuela had no idea what was going on. While the social media and the news channels were touting a revolution, in Caracas life went on as normal on the military bases and for the rest of Venezuela. Guaidó's attempt a coup d'état, for the most part, was just another demonstration that is all too common in Caracas...

One the day of Guaidó's publicity stunt Nicolás Maduro was strangely absent until late in the day with rumors abounding that he had left or was leaving the country. Did his Cuban bodyguards take Guaidó's actions seriously and isolate Maduro until the all-clear was given? Maybe... I am sure the Caucasian-looking Russian speakers on the streets of Caracas in Venezuelan National Guard uniforms were keeping Maduro's security team and others informed on all the developments with Guaidó's fiasco...

If Nicolás Maduro had planned to leave Venezuela is a matter for debate and only a select few know the facts. Maybe some of the passengers on the Bombardier Global Express that landed at 8 pm that evening at the airport in Maiquetía after a direct flight from Moscow would know the answer, who knows. Did the passengers of that plane meet with Maduro and clarify to him that he was not leaving the country, again, who knows. But Maduro is still in power and in the following days was seen dancing with his supporters and parading with the military.

For the past few months, there have been rumors and news reports about an imminent invasion of Venezuela by U.S. forces and its allies, even Eric Prince the former owner of the now-defunct Blackwater got in on the act asking for 5000 mercenaries to take the country from Maduro ... All this sounds cool and is good for publicity, ratings, and likes on social media but in reality, is it feasible or complete fantasy, I lean towards the latter...

The Ground

Venezuela, unlike Iraq, Afghanistan, and Syria, etc. is a hilly and heavily vegetated country with limited roads in many parts of the country. For most to comprehend Venezuela's terrain from a military point of view you want to be thinking Vietnam not Iraq. Venezuela's terrain is ideal for guerrilla warfare as heavily equipped conventional troops and security forces will be channeled for ambushes on limited routes and the abundant vegetation will provide ample cover for attackers. The Colombian military and security forces have been trying for years to control their borders with Venezuela but still today most of those areas are lawless badlands controlled by narcos, guerrillas and gangsters.

As for the cities such as Caracas... To clear and control Caracas militarily would be a huge challenge due to its terrain, limited main roads and its abundance of favelas/barrios. Most of the favelas/barrios are controlled by their own well-armed gangs and any outsiders entering the maze of alleyways are targeted. For the issues of operating in such environments take a look at how the Brazilian security forces work in the favelas of Rio and Sao Paulo. For troops that are not trained specifically to operate in that environment, are not fit enough, and don't know their way around, they would be chewed up and, if lucky, spat out...

The Population

Do most Venezuelans support the opposition? Well, I think they -

like everyone else - would support someone who would give them a better quality of life but are Venezuelans willing to fight for it... I think not... Yes, they will turn up to rallies, wave their flags and share their photos and videos on social media but, when the evening comes, and it starts to get dark they go home... Their priority like most in the Caribbean and Latin America is earning enough money to live, drink, fuck and party. What else do you need in life...?

From a military and cultural perspective, one of the huge differences between the wars in the Middle East and a potential war in Venezuela is the religion of the populations. While most in the U.S. and Europe have little cultural connection with the Muslims that have been killed in the wars in the Middle East, I think there would be a lot more public outrage against any military actions if Hispanic Catholics were being shot, bombed, killed and classed as collateral damage.

The Opposition

Juan Guaidó seems to have the support of the U.S. and their allies but not the people of Venezuela. Guaidó and his people all seem to be photogenic, wealthy and educated people whereas Nicolás Maduro was a bus driver and Hugo Chávez a career soldier, both from humble backgrounds and I don't think either of them would ever make the front cover of Vogue Magazine...

I don't think its difficult to see why most Venezuelans can relate more to Maduro and his predecessor Chávez than they can to Guaidó. I think Guaidó's opposition is more in tune drumming up donations with Miami's, Washington DC's and New York's socialites than fighting what would be a very dirty war.

Blackwater's 5000

If anyone with any military experience or knowledge can actually think they could seriously take control of a country like Venezuela with only 5000 well trained and equipped troops, I would say they must be delusional. If anyone was to think, these days, that they could raise a 5000 strong mercenary force to take control of a country like Venezuela, I would say they must be smoking crack.

• The now-defunct Blackwater was a security company that supplied guards to the U.S. Department of Defense, they were not a mercenary force. They operated within U.S. guidelines for the U.S. government.

• Blackwater did not engage in offensive front-line operations; they were a security company.

• Blackwater / Xe Services / Academi was reportedly in charge of running the training for the U.S.'s counternarcotics program in Afghanistan... Their achievements are questionable as we all know opium production in Afghanistan is booming...

• Blackwater/Xe Services/Academi has contracted to supply troops for Saudi Arabia's war in Yemen, which with all the money Saudi is spending is not going their way.

• To arm and equip a large mercenary force without government backing would require violating numerous international laws including arms trafficking to start with.

• Security companies operating in Iraq and Afghanistan etc. have to some degree had protection from prosecution for any shootings etc. they have been involved in, but guards have been held accountable and jailed for using what has been deemed excessive force. Anyone that follows military events and news will know that there are regular soldiers from the U.S. and U.K. being charged or are in jail for incidents that took place while on active duty. So, let's say hypothetically a mercenary force is involved in offensive operations where there are civilians killed, just your regular collateral damage which has to be expected in a war. These days do you think for a second no-one will try to prosecute these mercenaries for using excessive force, human rights violations, etc. etc. And when these guys return to their countries and have to face the legal ramifications of their actions do you think the company that hired them will be paying their legal bills? I think we all know the answer to that one...

• On a basic level, again when security companies are working in Iraq and Afghanistan on government contracts, they have access to medical and life insurance for their guards, not so with mercenary operations. Trying to get decent insurance for armed international close protection work is extremely expensive if not impossible to get, so how will they insure a mercenary operation that will undoubtedly be taking casualties. Repatriating bodies takes a lot of logistics and is expensive, from a business perspective it's far better to bury in place... Decent medical and aftercare for those wounded would again be expensive... I strongly suggest you check the fine print and validity of any medical or life insurance policies if you decide to partake in such adventures...

I have already heard that security companies are recruiting for operations in Venezuela, sure this makes good bar talk over a few beers but anything more than that, I would say find something constructive to focus on...

Armed Groups

In addition to the Venezuelan police, army, national guard and intelligence services there are an array of foreign forces who have been training there for years. The Russians have been highlighted recently, but also the Chinese, North Koreans and Hezbollah are active within the country. There are numerous photos online of Southeast Asians in Venezuelan military and their own national military uniforms. Will these foreign soldiers fight for Venezuela in the event of an invasion, well, I think it's in their interests to do so.

There are many videos poking fun at the Venezuelan Militias online but in a guerrilla war in the tight alleys of the favelas anyone putting lead in your general direction can cause casualties. At the other extreme, within the Venezuelan Armed forces, they are well trained, equipped and motivated troops that have been preparing for a foreign invasion for a long time.

I recently wrote an article about some of the main narco and terrorist organizations within Venezuela, and there are more that I will be writing about in the future.

Within Venezuela, as within all narco-states, parts of the country are controlled by armed gangs of terrorists, criminals or as they are locally known "Colectivos" who to some extent are operating with the consent of the government. In many places, these armed gangs outnumber and are better armed and paid than the local police and military forces.

This is where from a strategic perspective credit needs to be given to the former Venezuelan President Hugo Chávez because by arming, funding and facilitating these armed gangs he bought the government an unofficial army. These gangs are well organized, can operate independently and are embedded within their communities and what they are lacking in conventional military discipline and skills they compensate for with brutality and violence.

Venezuela is a very violent country where death and killing is a way of life for many, those within the gangs and colectivos are used to taking risks, fighting and killing. They have an operational command structure and are controlled by their bosses in the Venezuelan prison system or their friends in the intelligence services. For a very dirty guerrilla war these rapists, kidnapers, and murderers would be very effective tools.

Conclusion

Hopefully, you can see from this article a war within Venezuela would be a very dirty fight, which from what I see most armies these days are not trained for, and they would not be able to operate effectively due to oversight by politically correct bureaucrats and politicians.

With elections in the U.S. coming up in November 2020 and the political scene in Western Europe in chaos will the powers that be, commit to a war in Venezuela that will cost the lives of many from all the sides directly involved, I think not, but I could be very wrong...

Could there be a military solution to removing the communist government of Venezuela, sure but people need to decide if they really want it to happen or just use the idea to promote themselves on social media...

An active measure to start with could be to position a U.S. Navy aircraft carrier in the Southern Caribbean and every night when the narco flights start coming and going from Venezuela to send up their fighter jets to blow them out the sky. This might have a much more serious effect on Venezuela's economy than all the official sanctions, but I am sure it would affect the U.S. economy as well....

APPENDIX 3: MEXICAN DRUG CARTELS IN VENEZUELA

At approximately 10:15 pm on the 28th of April 2019 a Cessna 208 light aircraft made an emergency and unannounced landing at José Leonardo Chirinos International Airport in the city of Coro, Falcon State, Venezuela.

The plane had Mexican papers, the pilot "Rafael Guadalupe Rochar Venite", who was captured, was a Mexican national and they had just flown from Tijuana, MX. Of the four people on board, two escaped; the pilot and a passenger "Francisco Javier Denis Bueña" were captured by the airport security staff. The local media stated the plane was carrying contraband gasoline. The intended destination in Venezuela for this Cessna from Tijuana is unknown but we can say without a doubt it was heading for one of the estimated 2000 unofficial landing strips cut into the remote bush, or on the multitude of disused farms or more overtly, with government blessings, on straight and well and maintained stretches of road.

The nightly arrivals and departures of flights from Mexico are common, this one made the media since it landed at an international airport... A "Beechcraft 90 King Air" was found in 2018 in the bush in Zulia State, which borders Colombia. Again, it was flown and operated by Mexicans. If detained by the Venezuelan police or military those on board are usually released quickly without media coverage, no doubt for a fee... And as for the Venezuelan Air Forces order to shoot down Narco flights, well if you pay, you fly....

Here I have mentioned two planes that have made unexpected landings but we can be sure many more have crashed and disappeared into the jungles, forests or at sea while making the hazardous flights over Central America loaded with gasoline on their way south and drugs on their way back north. The pilots I have spoken to have explained that these night flights, landings, takeoffs, and evading radar require skilled pilots who must be receiving a standard of training that is above what's offered at most commercial flight schools.

The Mexican Cartels operate differently in Venezuela than in other countries... In Venezuela, they have representatives in residence who cut the deals with those from the Venezuelan military and intelligence services that run and coordinate the drug trade within the country. The Mexicans don't control territory or have to fight rival Cartels for influence or access to routes, for the Narcos and the like, Venezuela is a country where everyone gets along...

Hopefully, this article will help to highlight the fact that Venezuela, as I stated in my previous articles, is a Narco state, to say the very least. With the recent fiasco of a failed coup by the opposition leader "Juan Guaidó," the Venezuelan government are in a strong position to stay in power for the foreseeable future. In a recent article (How the Venezuelan intelligence service defeated the CIA: http://thesaker.is/how-the-venezuelan-intelligence-service-defeated-the-cia/) the Romanian military analyst "Valentin Vasilescu" detailed how the Venezuelan counterintelligence service "SEBIN" orchestrated Guaidó's failed coup attempt just to suck in the US Central Intelligence Agency, chew them up and spit them out in a humiliating intelligence defeat... I would say Vasilescu's opinions are about right.

So, the communists stay in power in Venezuela, and the opposition cry about their country, while living the Miami lifestyle in the U.S.. What's does this mean for the other countries in the region? The countries bordering Venezuela are useful to the Narco trade and have established protocols. Those at risk from the influences of the Cartels are the islands and countries of the Caribbean. Be it for trafficking routes, markets to sell, locations to launder money or to hide out, the Caribbean offers locations with poor security structures, corruptible governments and officials. But, if everyone is happy and making money, it's not really a problem, is it...?

APPENDIX 4: VENEZUELAN GOLD TRAFFICKING

In this chapter, I am going to explain a little about the Venezuelan gold trafficking business and those involved. For those in the close protection and international security world, the jewelry, gem and precious metals industry, can be a source of serious clients with an array of business and personal issues, that can require professional bodyguards, security consultants and investigators to help manage.

The gold business in general is a haven for scammers, money launderers, traffickers, criminals and terrorists. Its definitely a place where unsuspecting investors or greedy buyers can get themselves into a lot of trouble and lose a lot of money very quickly.

One of my main rules when providing protection services is not to trust the client's judgment, especially when they believe they are going to be making big money from a deal that might be slightly shady. The reason I know such deals could be shady is because the clients came to me in the first place, people won't pay for serious protection and investigations unless there is a need.

Another one of my rules, is that if I think the situation is shady and the clients don't want to take my advice then they are on their own... I will happily sit back and watch them crash and burn if they unnecessarily expose myself, or my associates to the risk of violence or being involved in illegal activities.

When you read through this chapter you will see there are some very serious and dangerous players involved in the illegal Venezuelan gold trafficking business alone, which spreads throughout Latin and North America, the Caribbean, Europe, Africa and the

Middle East. The same can be said for the international gold business in general where legitimate traders and buyers must be very careful to ensure the gold they are buying is not from conflict zones, sanctioned countries or being sold to launder money.

As part of your threat assessment, you need to know who could possibly be targeting your client and how they could cause problems. With clients in the Jewelry industry their main threats may not be physical assault or assassination, unless they have ripped someone off, and even then, professionals would want their funds returned before "offing" your client, and maybe you as well... Scams, extortion, robberies, honey traps and kidnapping are all potential risks that need to be considered.

You also need to ensure you know who your clients are... If you take on what you believe to be a legitimate contract and end up providing protection or transportation services to criminal or terrorist groups you can end up with a lot of problems, including legal issues with law enforcement etc... And, if during those legal issues the valuable assets you were escorting get seized and confiscated, don't be surprised if the bad guys hold you accountable, and expect you and your family to refund their losses in one way or another...

Venezuelan Crisis

After the United States and the Venezuelan oppositions failed coup attempt, on the Government of Nicolas Maduro on April 30th, 2019, life went back to normal in the chaos of Venezuela. Not only has life gone back to normal, but for many in the world of organized crime and trafficking, things are booming. The Narcos and the traffickers also know that as long as they pay their dues and cooperate with the Maduro Government, they are untouchable by law enforcement be it from the United States or Western Europe.

The trafficking routes established between the coastal towns - and organized crime hubs - of Guiria and Macuro in Sucre State, Venezuela and the coastal towns of Chaguaramas and Woodbrook in Trinidad & Tobago is a blatant example of how unconcealed the trafficking is.

The kidnapping of women aged between 14 years to 25 years is on the rise all over Venezuela, and in Trinidad & Tobago they pay up to $1000 USD per woman. The human trafficking business in Venezuela is controlled by the Bolivarian Intelligence and Bolivarian National Guard. They have found that controlling human trafficking is an easy and profitable way of making money.

The Venezuelan drug trafficking business is booming between the coastal towns in Sucre State and Trinidad & Tobago. Venezuelan Coast Guard, Bolivarian National Guard, Bolivarian Intelligence and Military Intelligence are all profiting as are members of the Trinidad & Tobago Coast Guard and political figures.

It's understood the Trinidad & Tobago Coast Guard is not well equipped, not well paid, it lacks manpower and is corrupt. They intercept boats with illegal immigrants coming from Venezuela but do not touch or chase the ones carrying drugs and women that will be working or sold as prostitutes.

Gold Trafficking

Venezuela's third-largest export is gold, and the country's gold production is controlled by the military. Reuters reported that officially 20 tons of national reserve gold and 23 tons of mined gold were taken to Istanbul, Turkey in 2018. In November 2018, U.S. President Donald Trump signed an executive order to "ban U.S. persons from dealing with entities and individuals involved with 'corrupt or deceptive' gold sales from Venezuela."

Since the U.S. imposed sanctions on Venezuela and due to the dilapidated state of the oil industry, the Venezuelan government, with the help of organized crime groups, have found the gold business a nice and quick way of making money.

In 2016 the Venezuelan government foreseeing economic and political problems in the future created the Arco Minero del Orinoco area, that covers the states of Bolívar, Amazonas and Delta Amacuro. The area covered by the Arco Minero del Orinoco is rich in mineral resources; experts estimate 7,000 tons of gold, copper, diamonds, uranium, coltan, iron, bauxite and other mineral reserves. Environmental and human rights groups immediately raised concerns about the potential destruction and pollution of the environment and the exploitation of those who would be working in and supporting the mining operations.

At the moment the main areas of activity are El Callao, Tumeremo and Las Cristinas in Bolívar State and the main commodity is gold. The area covered by Arco Minero del Orinoco can be classed as one of the most lawless, dangerous and corrupt places on earth. Nothing that happens there is clean, life is cheap, the money is dirty, and business is booming.

The main players overseeing the Venezuelan gold business are the usual suspects... President Nicolas Maduro, his son Nicolás Maduro Guerra and his wife Cilia Flores. Two of Cilia Flores' nephews were arrested in Haiti in 2015 by the U.S. DEA, on drug trafficking charges and sentenced to 18 years in U.S. prison. There is Tareck El Aissami who is wanted by the US authorities, a serving Venezuelan politician, the Minister of Industries and National Production, and also reportedly a Hezbollah liaison. And then, of course, there is the GNB (Bolivarian National Guard), FANB (Bolivarian army and Bolivarian navy) and SEBIN (National Intelligence Service).

Other players and foot soldiers in the Venezuelan gold business include:

· **Colombian guerrillas:** They operate will the full support from the Venezuelan regime; it's believed that there are more than 2000 well-armed and well-equipped guerrilla members performing security activities and gold extraction in Bolívar state. The direct order (coming from President Maduro) to the Bolivarian Armed

Forces, is to support and help them with everything from weapons, ammunition, uniforms, vehicles and even transporting them on helicopters that belong to the Air Force or Army. Every single military base in Bolívar state has the order to assist and shelter guerrilla group members.

· **Venezuelan gang members:** Gang members from such groups as Pranes are into almost every dirty way of making money; extortion, killing, kidnapping, drug trafficking, human trafficking, etc. And now they are into the gold business with the blessing from high-up officials from the Venezuelan regime. They're responsible for at least 1000 murders just in Bolívar state. Since last year, the Colombian guerrillas have been taking over their territory, which is turning the situation into a medium scale war.

· **Local gold mafia:** The gold business in Bolívar state is old and established. Most of the businessmen from Bolívar state trade in gold, they're well-armed, but they prefer to stay low profile. You can see them and their people at their gold shops in almost every single town and in Puerto Ordaz city.

· **Syrian nationals:** Recently, many people from Syria have been moving to Venezuela and establishing themselves in Bolívar state and in the gold business; they come will full support from Tareck El Aissami.

· **Hezbollah:** Hezbollah is performing activities related to gold extraction and trafficking. The terrorist group has a large international network and is making a lot of money in Venezuela; the gold ends up in Turkey, UAE, and even Syria.

Mixed in with these groups are the Chinese, Turks, and Russians who are operating in the Venezuelan gold business and trying to stay clean and out of the turf wars. The Venezuelan gold is being trafficked regionally by air or river into Colombia, Brazil, Guyana, and Suriname where it can be mixed in and marked as locally produced and then moved internationally to Turkey, Tanzania, and UAE, etc.

Most of Bolívar and the neighboring States are covered in jungle, and thick forest and the only way of getting into many towns is by air. The bush pilots in the area are the best-paid pilots in Venezuela, all they do is fly logistics, food, weapons, gold, prostitutes, medicines and anything else needed.

The Venezuelan gold business brings with it chaos, crime, kidnapping, murder, well-armed gang members and guerrillas but it's booming because of the vast amount of money that is being made by those involved. The profits from the Venezuelan gold business go to sustain the affluent lifestyles of those in the upper echelons, but also to corrupt officials and influential people in the region and internationally, who can help facilitate this criminal industry, which these days is Venezuela's main export.

Conclusion

There is a lot more to providing protective services than just supplying bodies to react to the threats of robbery, assault and kidnappings. The aim needs to be to prevent and avoid any potential problematic or hostile situations and to do this you must understand the environments you're working in and the specific issues your clients could encounter.

Many clients don't realize the problems and threats they could be exposing themselves, their employees and their families to, until you explain certain realities to them. Some clients take the advice seriously and will work with you to put workable procedures and plans in place, and others will dismiss your advice as just paranoid scaremongering. How you deal with your clients, their attitudes and decisions, is solely up to you, and hopefully dealing with their problems are worth what you're getting paid.

ORLANDO "ANDY" WILSON

Orlando has worked internationally at all levels of the specialist security and investigation industry for over 35 years. Over the years, he has become accustomed to the types of complications that can occur, when dealing with international law enforcement agencies and the problem of dealing with kidnapping, organized crime and Mafia groups.

His experience in the international security business began in 1988 when he enlisted in the British army at 17 years of age and volunteered for a 22-month frontline, operational tour in Northern Ireland in an Infantry unit, 4 Platoon, 1 WFR. He then joined his unit's Reconnaissance Platoon, with which he undertook intensive training in small-unit warfare.

Since leaving the British army in 1993, his time spent working in Eastern Europe in the 1990s gave him firsthand experience of the operational procedures of organized criminals and Mafia groups from the former Soviet Union. In addition, he had the opportunity to oversee criminal cases that have been the first of their kind in their respective country. His operations in Mexico training tactical police teams put him in a unique position to understand the war on Narco-Terrorism.

His continuous and ongoing projects focusing on kidnap and ransom prevention in South America, the Caribbean and West Africa have given him the knowledge to formulate practical programs to counter the kidnapping threat.

Orlando is a published author, writer, photographer and has been interviewed by numerous international TV and media outlets on topics ranging from kidnapping, organized crime to maritime piracy. He had his first article published in 1997 in an association magazine and his first book in 2012. He has been interviewed by media outlets ranging from the Professional Mariner Magazine, Newsweek Serbia, Newsweek en Espanol, GrupoMilenio, Mundo-Fox, The New York Times, the BBC, Soldier of Fortune Magazine and others.

Orlando's diverse and continuous operational experience enables him to provide no-nonsense professional services and training programs. His operational investigation and close protection procedures are cutting edge and the most effective commercially available. He is also a founding member and operations manager of Risks Incorporated.

OTHER BOOKS BY ORLANDO

These Books are Available on Amazon!

Non-Fiction Manuals

• Social Navigation: A Practical Survival Guide for Human Interactions

• Counter Insurgency Operations: A tactical Guide for Law Enforcement

• Intelligence Gathering: Front Line HUMINT Considerations

• Caribbean Security Threats: A threat assessment for the islands of the Caribbean

• Gun Range Management: A Guide for Range Managers, Range Safety Officers & Firearms Instructors

• Investigative Journalist Security: Staying Alive to Tell the Truth

• Threat Assessments for Close Protection & Security Management

• Protecting Your Loved Ones: Security Awareness for Parents & Adults

• Close Protection: Luxury & Hostile Environments

• Tactical Pistolcraft for Protective Operations

• Home & Office Security: Protection of Residencies & Businesses

• Travel Security: Personal Travel & Vehicle Security

• Counter Terrorism: Terrorist Attack Response

• Kidnap & Ransom: The Essentials of Kidnapping Prevention

Crime Fiction

• The Shoot: An Assassin's World

• Vengeance: The Art of Pain

• The Collectors: Death is Easy, Life is Hard

• Reglas Mexicanas: A Life Without Pain, Is Not A Life

Photo Books

• Athens Lockdown 2020 in Pictures

• Wandering in Serbia

• Vigilantes of Imo – Nigerian Vigilante Life in Pictures

www.ingramcontent.com/pod-product-compliance
Lightning Source LLC
Chambersburg PA
CBHW070431180526
45158CB00017B/963